Growing Green

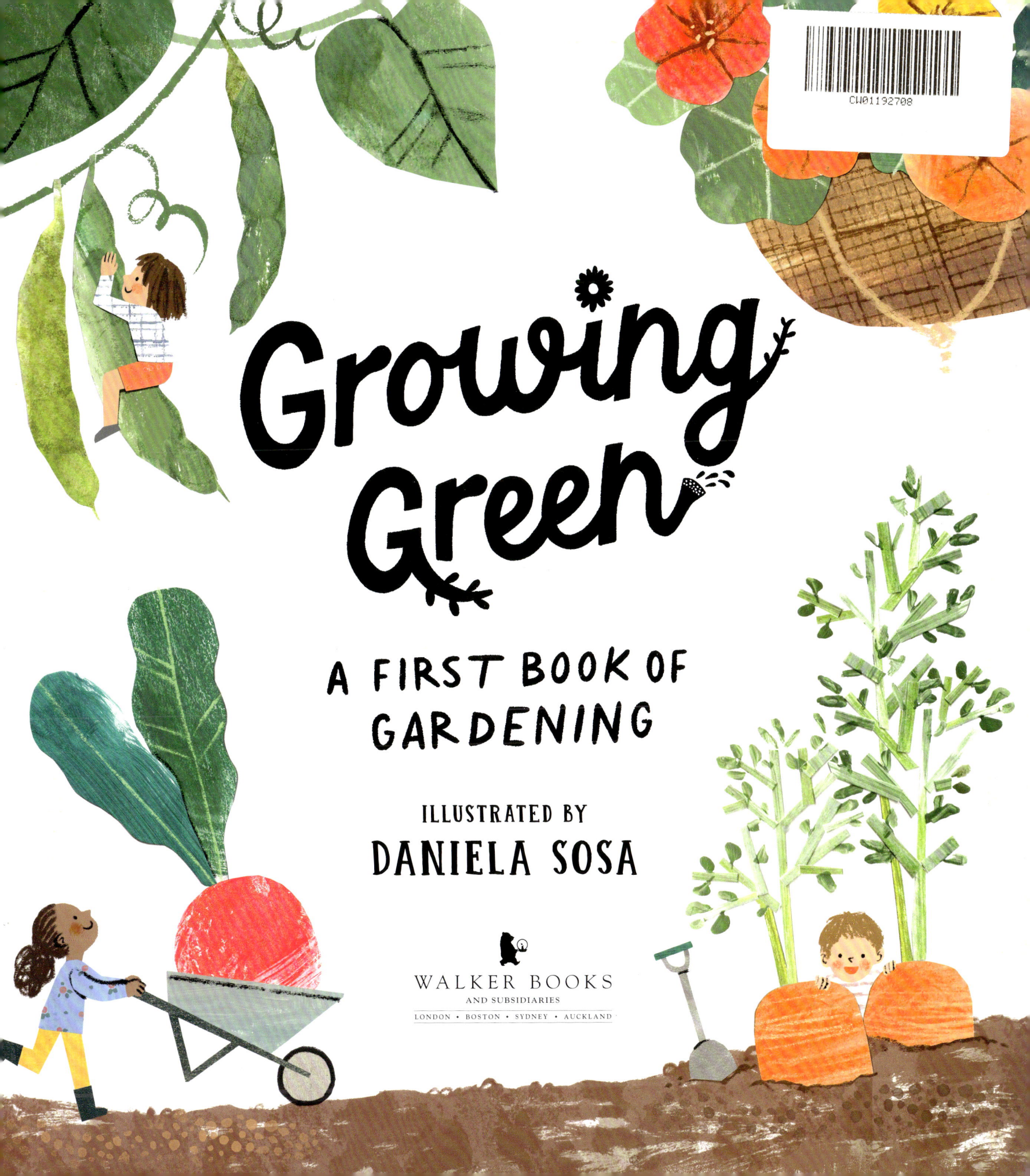

A FIRST BOOK OF GARDENING

ILLUSTRATED BY
DANIELA SOSA

WALKER BOOKS
AND SUBSIDIARIES
LONDON · BOSTON · SYDNEY · AUCKLAND

CONTENTS

Getting started	5	
Strawberries in wellies	6	
Tomatoes in hanging baskets	8	
Dwarf French beans	10	
New potatoes	12	
Carrots	14	
Sweetcorn	16	
Pumpkins	18	

Avocado pits	20	
Celery bottoms	22	
Radishes	24	
Cressheads	25	
Tin can herb garden	26	
Endless salad leaves	28	
Nasturtiums	29	
Sunflowers	30	

GETTING STARTED

Gardening is great! It's a brilliant (often) outdoor activity and you can really get your hands dirty! Planting a seed, caring for it and watching it grow is easy and fun – and there's nothing more delicious than a juicy, ripe strawberry you've grown yourself.

You'll need some basic kit: compost (make sure it's peat-free to preserve natural habitats), a trowel and garden fork, a watering can, labels and garden twine – and, of course, seeds! You may want to wear gardening gloves, especially if you need to do any weeding. You don't have to buy everything, though. Raid your recycling: fruit punnets make great trays for seedlings, and yoghurt pots can be used instead of plant pots (remember to make drainage holes). If you ask an adult to pierce some holes in the lid of a plastic drinks bottle, you'll have a home-made watering can, and you can make your own compost from kitchen scraps and garden waste.

You don't need a lot of space – you don't even need a garden. There are projects in this book that you can do on your kitchen worktop and lots more that can be grown on windowsills and in pots. It's amazing how much you can grow on a balcony and if you have access to an allotment, the sky's the limit.

So why grow your own fruit and vegetables? Well, being self-sufficient is good for the planet. It creates less plastic waste than shop-bought veggies, reduces food miles and, best of all, means you get to choose what you want to grow and eat.

Look after your plants well. Water them when the soil around the base begins to feel dry. When you need to move seedlings to a bigger pot, handle them with care. If you are planting seedlings outdoors, harden them up by taking them outside during the day for a few days to get them used to a different climate.

Whatever you choose to grow, have fun and enjoy growing green!

STRAWBERRIES IN WELLIES

YOU WILL NEED:

- An old pair of wellies
- Screwdriver/drill/scissors
- Stones/gravel
- Compost
- 4 x strawberry plants
- Trowel
- Plant food

Strawberries are sweet, delicious and easy to grow, and can give you a good crop of fruit for 3–4 years. Plant in April or May and you should see a healthy harvest from June and July onwards.

SEASON: Spring, summer & autumn

TIME: About 3 months

ENVIRONMENT: Outdoors

HOW TO GROW:

1 Remove the insoles from the welly boots and ask your adult to pierce holes in the bottoms using a screwdriver or a drill.

2 Create a shallow layer of stones or gravel inside the boots to help drainage, then fill both wellies nearly to the top with compost.

3 Get your adult to make a slit halfway up one side of each boot.

4 Now, plant a seedling in the top of each boot. The base of the plant, where the stalks start, should be at the same level as the soil.

5 Get your hands dirty and scoop out enough soil from the side pockets to plant another strawberry in each.

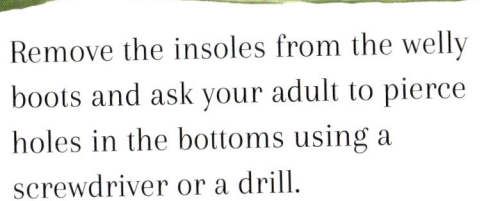

6 Make sure that your wellies are in a sunny spot and water them every day. Feed them once a week with plant food.

7 When you see fruit, you may want to cover your plants with a bit of netting to keep the birds from snacking!

8 Check your plants every day and harvest them when your strawberries look big, juicy and red-ripe. Eat them straight away!

7

TOMATOES IN HANGING BASKETS

If you don't have much space, a great way to grow tomatoes is in a hanging basket. You can grow them from seed or buy plants from your local garden centre in late spring/early summer.

YOU WILL NEED:

- A hanging basket
- A liner (a circle cut from an old compost bag is ideal)
- Compost
- Tomato plants (make sure you use a "tumbling" variety)
- Plant food

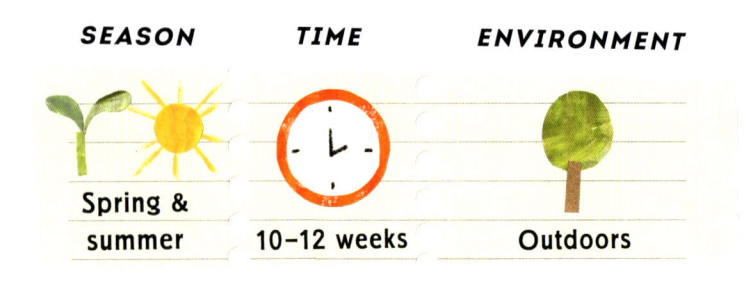

SEASON: Spring & summer

TIME: 10–12 weeks

ENVIRONMENT: Outdoors

HOW TO GROW:

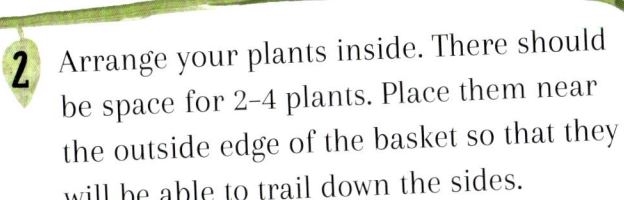

1 Line your basket with plastic and fill it about ⅔ of the way up with compost. Make 5 or 6 small holes in the bottom for drainage.

2 Arrange your plants inside. There should be space for 2-4 plants. Place them near the outside edge of the basket so that they will be able to trail down the sides.

4 Gently tap down the compost, water in the plants and hang your basket in a sunny spot.

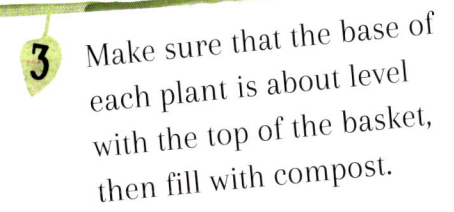

3 Make sure that the base of each plant is about level with the top of the basket, then fill with compost.

5 Water regularly and feed with plant food every 2 weeks once they start to flower.

6 Within a few weeks you will begin to see tomatoes. Check for ripe fruit every few days and gently pull them off the plant.

DID YOU KNOW?
Tomato plants were first grown for food by the Aztecs in America. Every year in August, 20,000 people gather in the Spanish town of Buñol for an epic tomato-throwing festival. More than 100 tonnes of over-ripe tomatoes are thrown in the streets!

DWARF FRENCH BEANS

Dwarf French beans are really easy to grow. They like a sunny spot with good drainage and can be sown in yoghurt pots with holes in the bottom. Seeds can be planted indoors in April and transplanted outside in May or sown straight into the ground from May onwards.

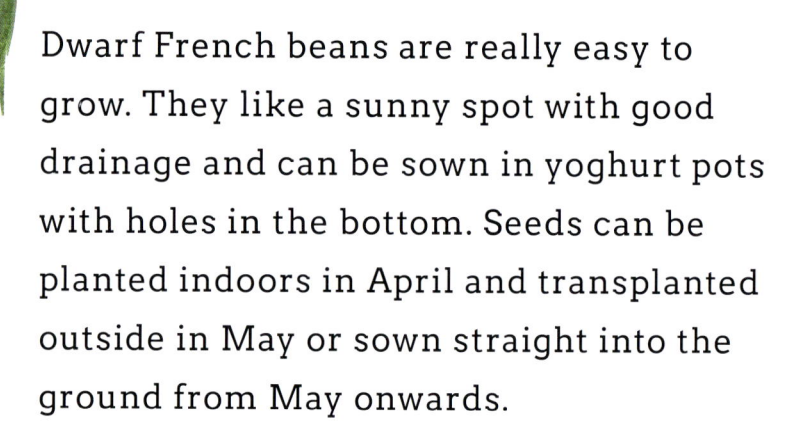

YOU WILL NEED:

- Small pots
- Compost
- Seeds
- Labels and a pen
- Large pots (or a vegetable patch)
- A trowel
- Garden canes and string

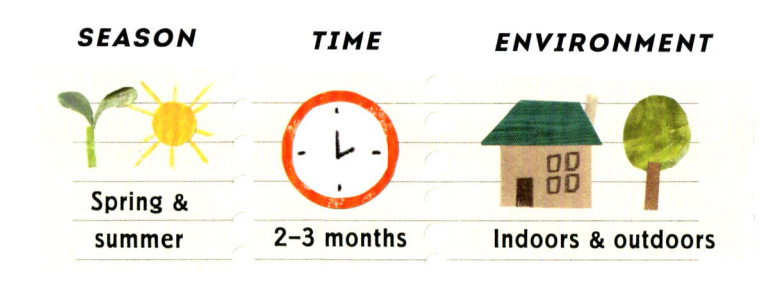

SEASON: Spring & summer

TIME: 2–3 months

ENVIRONMENT: Indoors & outdoors

HOW TO GROW:

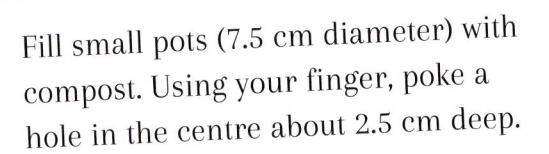

BEANS

1 Fill small pots (7.5 cm diameter) with compost. Using your finger, poke a hole in the centre about 2.5 cm deep.

2 Drop one bean seed into each hole, cover with soil and water well.

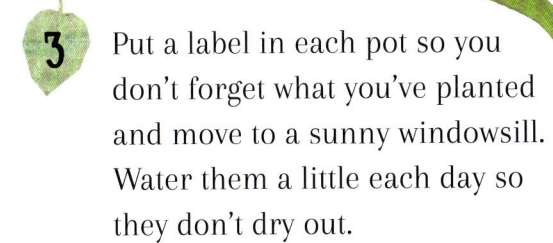

3 Put a label in each pot so you don't forget what you've planted and move to a sunny windowsill. Water them a little each day so they don't dry out.

5 Choose where to plant them – you can transfer them to a large pot or straight into the soil. Use your trowel to dig a hole the same size as your small pot.

4 Seeds will germinate in about a week and you should see green shoots emerge. After 3 weeks your seedlings should be ready to plant outside.

6 Carefully tap out the seedling and place in the hole. Fill in any space around it with soil or compost.

7 As they grow, support the plants by creating a "bean cage" out of garden canes (or sticks) and string. Carefully wrap the plants around it.

8 Pick your beans as soon as the pods are swollen and ready to harvest. More beans should grow if you harvest them regularly.

NEW POTATOES

Digging your own new potatoes out of the ground makes them much, much tastier than shop-bought spuds. They're fun to grow in either a vegetable patch or a large pot. You can also get special growbags if you don't have much space in your garden.

YOU WILL NEED:

- Seed potatoes
- Old egg boxes
- A trowel
- A vegetable patch (or a large pot and compost)
- Labels and a pen
- A garden fork

SEASON: Spring & summer

TIME: 10–12 weeks

ENVIRONMENT: Outdoors

HOW TO GROW:

1 In early February, buy some seed potatoes. Six will give you plenty of potatoes! Make sure you buy "early" potatoes to grow small, new potatoes.

2 With the "eyes" (little buds of growth) at the top, put one seed potato in each pocket of the egg box. Leave on a sunny windowsill until they start to sprout. This is known as "chitting".

3 Towards the end of March, the soil should be warm enough to plant out your chitted potatoes.

4 If planting them in a container, make sure that it can drain easily. Fill it with compost to about 2 cm from the top, then plant your chits 10 cm deep.

5 Label them and give them a really good water.

6 The potato plants will grow quickly and you should begin to see shoots after about 3–5 weeks.

7 When the shoots are 10 cm above ground level, you need to mound the soil up around the stalks. This is called "earthing up" and it helps you get a really good crop.

8 In June and July, the plants will begin to flower. When they have finished flowering, they should be ready to harvest.

9 To harvest, use a garden fork to dig under the plant and lever up the crop. If you're using containers, you can just turn them upside down and help yourself!

CARROTS

Carrots can be grown for a good part of the year, from March to July. They are packed full of nutrients and can be grown in lots of colours – even purple and white!

SEASON: Spring, summer & autumn

TIME: 3–4 months

ENVIRONMENT: Outdoors

YOU WILL NEED:

- A vegetable patch or a large pot
- Compost
- A garden fork
- A rake
- Carrot seeds

HOW TO GROW:

1 If you are growing the carrots straight into your garden, you will need to dig the ground over to break up the soil and make sure that it is weed-free. You may want to get an adult to help you with this! If you're using big pots, fill the pots nearly to the top with compost.

2 Rake over the surface of the soil (or compost) and drag your finger through the soil to make a line (1 cm deep). If you are growing more than one row, make sure that they are 15–30 cm apart.

3 Sow the seeds into your groove, cover gently and water. Continue to water them every other day.

DID YOU KNOW?
Carrots are full of beta-carotene – this gives them their orange colour and turns into vitamin A in your body, which is really good for your eyesight.

4 When the seeds start to sprout, thin them out so that they are 5–7 cm apart.

5 If the tops of the carrots become visible above the ground, just cover them up with more soil or compost. Make sure to keep your carrots weed-free.

6 When the tops of the carrots measure about 2–3 cm across, it's time to dig them up. Simply grasp the base of the stalks and pull! If you have a huge crop, you can leave them in the ground until autumn.

SWEETCORN

Super-sweet corn on the cob tastes even more delicious when it's eaten fresh from your garden. Sown in April or May, it is best started indoors then planted out into large containers or straight into the ground. It likes a sunny but sheltered spot, so next to a wall would be a good place. It doesn't like to have its roots disturbed so is best sown in a cardboard tube, which can then be planted straight into the ground.

YOU WILL NEED:

- Toilet roll tubes
- Compost
- Sweetcorn seeds
- Labels and a pen
- A vegetable patch or a large pot
- A trowel

SEASON	TIME	ENVIRONMENT
Spring, summer & autumn	2–4 months	Indoors & outdoors

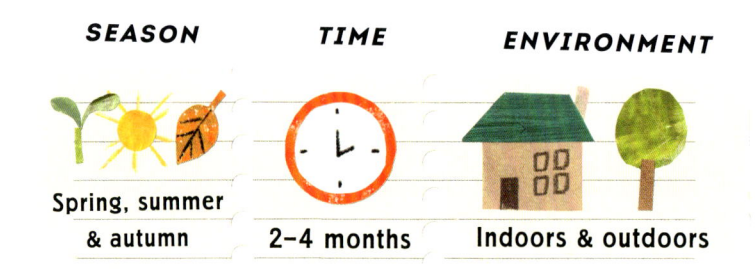

DID YOU KNOW?

There are about 800 kernels on each cob of corn!

HOW TO GROW:

1 Fill your toilet rolls nearly to the top with compost, water lightly and poke two holes (4 cm deep) in each with your finger.

2 Pop a seed in each hole, cover them over with compost and water gently. Label the tubes and leave them on a sunny windowsill.

3 When the seeds have germinated – usually after about 10 days – remove the weaker of the two seedlings.

5 Arrange your containers in blocks rather than a line, so that the plants will be successfully pollinated. Water once a week.

4 When all danger of frost has passed, and your seedlings look strong enough to transplant, plant them outside in large pots. If you are planting into a vegetable patch, you will need to keep them 60 cm apart.

6 After they have flowered, the cobs will begin to grow – inside protective leaves. You may need to water them more often at this stage.

7 When the "silks" at the top of the cobs begin to turn dark brown, your sweetcorn will be ready to harvest. Gently peel back the leaves and check that the kernels are bright yellow and plump.

8 To harvest, simply twist the cobs off the main stalk, pulling sharply.

PUMPKINS

Pumpkin seeds should be planted in late April or May to harvest your crop in time for Halloween. Pumpkins can take up a lot of space so you may need to plant these straight into the ground – though there are mini varieties available if you only have room for pots.

YOU WILL NEED:

- Pumpkin seeds
- Small pots or yoghurt pots with holes in the bottom
- Compost
- Labels and a pen
- A trowel
- Plant food

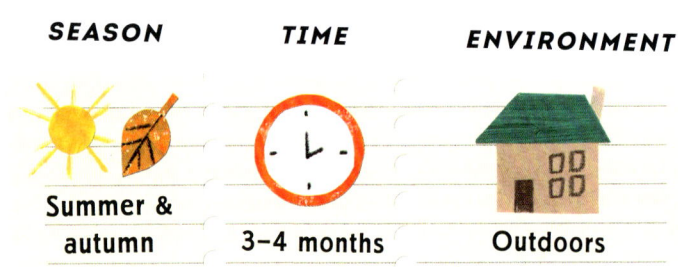

SEASON: Summer & autumn

TIME: 3–4 months

ENVIRONMENT: Outdoors

DID YOU KNOW?

The largest-ever pumpkin was grown in Italy in 2021. It weighed 1,226 kg, which is about the same as a small car!

HOW TO GROW:

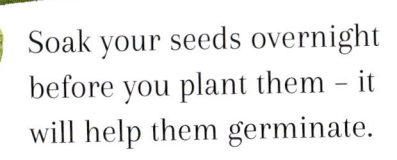

1. Soak your seeds overnight before you plant them – it will help them germinate.

2. Fill your pots nearly to the top with compost, water lightly and poke a hole (2 cm deep) in each with your finger.

3. Pop a seed in each hole, making sure that it points up, rather than lying on its flat side, and cover with compost.

4. Label your pots and put them on a warm sunny windowsill (or in a greenhouse if you have access to one).

5. Water them every couple of days and when they are about 10-15 cm tall, they should be ready to transplant into the garden. This should be from late May onwards.

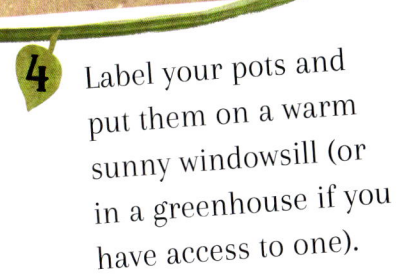

6. Dig a hole in your vegetable patch that is slightly bigger than your pot and put some more compost in the bottom. Carefully tip the seedling out, protecting the root growth.

7. Place it gently in the hole and then fill in any gaps around your plant with more compost. Water in gently.

8. You'll need to keep your pumpkins well watered throughout the summer and protect your plants from slugs.

9. When the pumpkins start to grow, feed your plant with plant food every 2 weeks. You may want to put a piece of cardboard or an old piece of wood underneath the pumpkins to stop them getting soggy and rotting.

10. The pumpkins will be ready to harvest when they are really colourful and the stems begin to crack. After you've cut them from the plant, leave them in the sun for a week so that their skins harden.

AVOCADO PITS

These can be grown all year round on a sunny windowsill in your home. They make lovely houseplants, but be aware that if you want to grow your own avocados to eat, it will take at least five years!

YOU WILL NEED:

- An avocado seed (pit)
- 3 toothpicks/cocktail sticks
- A clean jam jar
- A medium-sized pot
- Compost
- Plant food

HOW TO GROW:

1 The next time you're eating an avocado, ask an adult to carefully remove the seed with a knife. Wash it and leave to dry.

2 Holding the round end down, pierce the pit around the middle with the three cocktail sticks, spacing them equally, then balance it across the top of the jar.

9 Place it gently in the pot and, still holding the stem, add more soil until it reaches about a third of the way up the seed.

10 Pat the soil down to make sure that the seed is stable, then take out the toothpicks. Water it sparingly and feed it once a week with plant food.

SEASON All year round

TIME At least 5 years

ENVIRONMENT Indoors

DID YOU KNOW?
Avocados are incredibly high in potassium, which helps keep your heart healthy.

3 Add enough water to reach halfway up the pit.

4 Put the jar on a warm, sunny windowsill and change the water every 5 days to stop any algae growing.

5 After about 3–5 weeks, you should see some root growth developing.

6 After 7–8 weeks, you should see a shoot coming out of the top and the seed will split in half. By 10 weeks, you should have some leaves growing.

7 As long as the leaves look healthy you can keep it in the jam jar, but as soon as the leaves start to turn yellow or dry out, you need to transplant it to a plant pot.

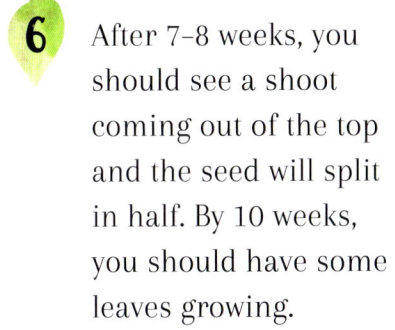

8 Half-fill a 15–20 cm plant pot with soil or compost. Very carefully lift the seed out of the jam jar, picking it up by the stem so that the pit itself doesn't split.

21

CELERY BOTTOMS

This is one of the easiest things that you can grow from kitchen scraps and can be grown on any windowsill. You can grow it outdoors in spring or autumn and anytime of the year indoors.

YOU WILL NEED:

- The bottom of a head of celery
- A small bowl
- Water
- A medium pot
- Compost

DID YOU KNOW?
Celery is a great source of antioxidants and has been used to treat toothache, sleeplessness and anxiety. Winners of athletic events in ancient Greece would be presented with a bunch of celery, much as modern-day winners would be given flowers!

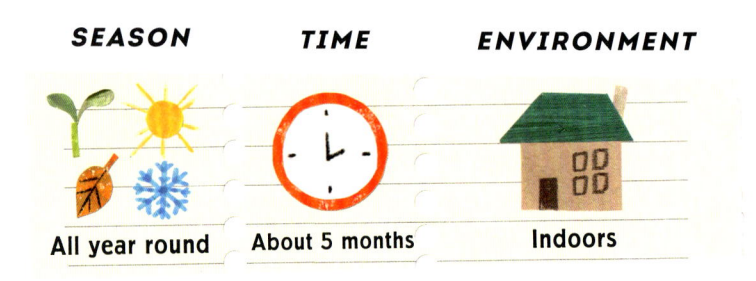

SEASON: All year round

TIME: About 5 months

ENVIRONMENT: Indoors

HOW TO GROW:

1. The next time anyone is cooking with celery in your house, ask an adult to cut the bottom off, leaving 5–8 cm of the stalks intact.

2. Fill a small bowl with 2.5 cm of water, then take 3 or 4 of the outer stems off the celery bottom and place it in the bowl.

3. Place the bowl on a sunny windowsill and change the water every 2–3 days to keep it fresh.

4. After about 6 days, you should be able to see growth in the centre of the celery bottom.

5. After about 2 weeks, roots should begin to form – usually at the sides.

6. When you see the roots (there may not be many) you can transfer it into a medium-large pot (about 20 cm across). Fill the pot with compost, then water it really well so that it is soggy.

7. Put the celery bottom on the top of the compost and add in another 2.5 cm of compost around it. Pat it down firmly, to secure the base.

8. Wait until your new plant reaches full size, then harvest the stalks.

23

RADISHES

These tasty round roots add colour and crunch to your lunch. They grow quickly and can be sown straight into the ground in the summer months.

SEASON — All year round

TIME — 4–8 weeks

ENVIRONMENT — Indoors & outdoors

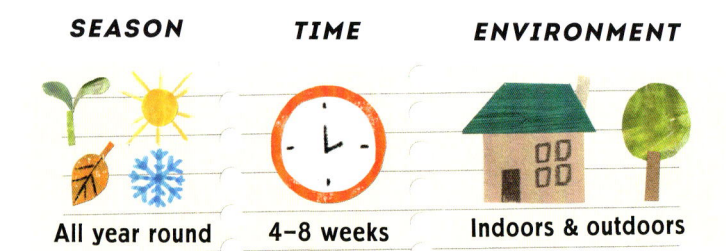

YOU WILL NEED:

- A large shallow pot or a vegetable patch
- A trowel
- A rake or small garden fork
- Radish seeds
- Labels and a pen

HOW TO GROW:

1 Make sure that your patch of earth or pot is completely weed-free before you start by digging out any weeds with a trowel.

2 Use a rake or fork to break up any large lumps of soil until you have a smooth, crumbly surface to plant in.

3 Draw a line in the soil with your trowel, making a groove about 1 cm deep.

4 Sprinkle the radish seeds thinly along the groove and cover with soil. (If you are sowing more than one line, make sure that the lines are 15 cm apart.)

5 Water the soil and as the seedlings grow, thin them out by removing the weaker ones. Leave 2.5 cm spaces between the remaining plants so that they have enough room to grow strongly.

6 After 4–6 weeks, you will begin to see radishes that are ready for eating. Pick them when they measure 2–3 cm across, before they grow too big and peppery.

CRESSHEADS

Cressheads can be grown all year round. They are quick, easy and lots of fun!

HOW TO GROW:

YOU WILL NEED:

- 6 empty eggshells
- An egg box
- Cotton wool
- Cress seeds
- Marker pens

SEASON: All year round
TIME: 5–7 days
ENVIRONMENT: Indoors

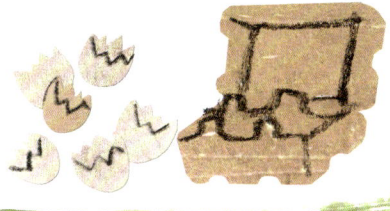

1 Whenever you have boiled eggs for breakfast, carefully clean out the shells really well and save them up in an old egg box, until you have a set of six.

2 Place a ball of cotton wool inside each of the empty shells and sprinkle a thin layer of cress seeds evenly across it.

3 Draw faces on each of the eggs. You can turn them into whatever you like – let your imagination run riot! When you're done, carefully water each eggshell.

4 Store them in a warm, sunny place. Keep the cotton wool moist and your cress should begin to grow.

5 After about 7 days, you should have lots of lovely hair on your egg-heads.

6 Give them a trim and enjoy the cress in a tasty sandwich.

TIN CAN HERB GARDEN

Growing herbs on a kitchen windowsill will help you cook with flavour. Most herbs are easy to grow, but basil, mint, parsley and coriander are all particularly quick to grow from seed.

SEASON	TIME	ENVIRONMENT
All year round	4-6 weeks	Indoors

YOU WILL NEED:

- Tin cans (lids removed and washed by an adult)
- A hammer and a nail
- Acrylic paints
- Compost
- Herb seeds
- A marker pen (or labels and a pen)
- An old plate or tray

HOW TO GROW:

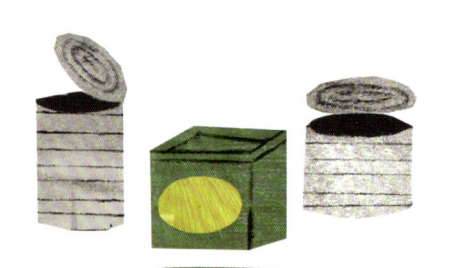

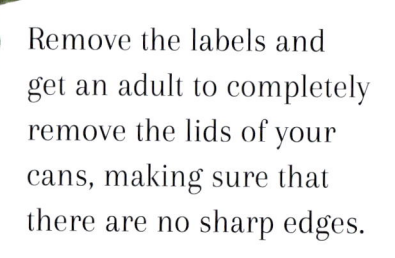

1. Remove the labels and get an adult to completely remove the lids of your cans, making sure that there are no sharp edges.

2. Ask them to use the hammer and nail to punch a few drainage holes into the bottom of the cans.

3. Wash the cans carefully and paint the outsides with acrylic paints, then leave to dry. You can make them as decorative as you like.

26

DID YOU KNOW?
Parsley is an excellent source of vitamins K and C – it can also help you get rid of bad breath smells!

10 For a continuous supply of herbs, you can add a few more seeds to the cans as you harvest.

9 After about 4–6 weeks, you should be able to start harvesting your herbs.

8 Continue watering whenever the compost begins to feel dry and after about a week, you should begin to see your seeds sprouting.

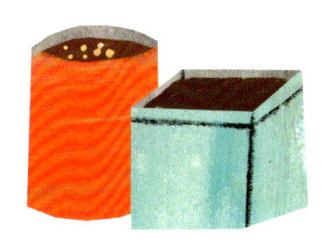

BASIL

4 You can use a marker pen to write what type of herb you are going to grow in each pot, or use plant labels.

5 Fill the cans with compost until it reaches about 1 cm from the top.

6 Choosing one type of herb for each can, sprinkle a few seeds evenly over the top of the compost.

7 Add a little more compost to cover up the seeds, then water them and set the cans down on an old plate or tray so that your windowsill doesn't get wet!

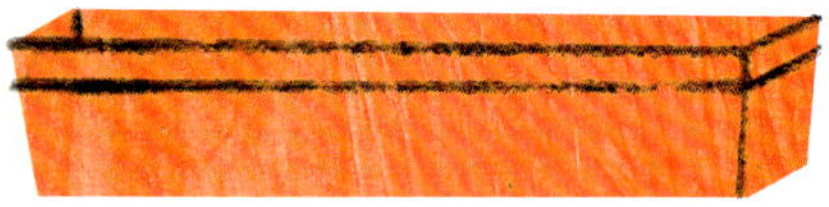

ENDLESS SALAD LEAVES

Salad leaves can be grown in a shallow pot on a sunny windowsill or balcony, in growbags or even straight into the ground in summer. Choose salad plants that have individual leaves (such as rocket or chard) and you can sow when you harvest for a continuous supply. Sow outdoors from March to August to harvest from June to September.

YOU WILL NEED:
- A wide, shallow container (or a vegetable patch)
- Compost
- A rake
- Salad seeds

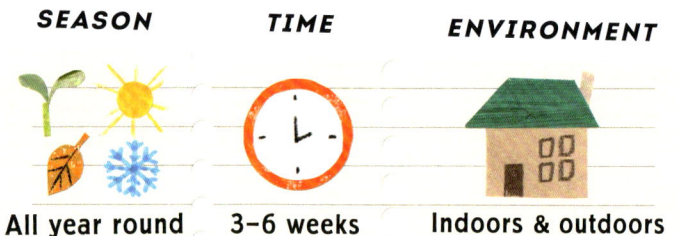

SEASON: All year round
TIME: 3–6 weeks
ENVIRONMENT: Indoors & outdoors

HOW TO GROW:

1. Fill your container nearly to the top with compost.

2. Rake over the surface so that it is even, then use your finger to draw straight lines in the soil, (1 cm deep and 10–15 cm apart).

3. Water well, then lightly sprinkle the seeds into the grooves, spacing them about 1 cm apart.

4. Cover very lightly with compost or soil and water regularly.

5. When the leaves are the right size to eat, cut them close to ground level. Be careful not to cut the heart of the plant, though, so that more leaves can grow.

6. Throughout the growing season, add more seeds to the rows for more crops to harvest.

NASTURTIUMS

Nasturtiums are bright and colourful with edible petals, leaves and seeds. They're easy to grow and don't mind bad weather. Seeds can be planted outside in the spring, after all chance of frost has passed. There are three types of nasturtium (low-growing, trailing and climbing), so make sure you select the right type for your space.

YOU WILL NEED:
- Nasturtium seeds
- A large pot (30 cm)
- Soil or compost

HOW TO GROW:

SEASON: Spring & summer
TIME: 6–9 weeks
ENVIRONMENT: Indoors & outdoors

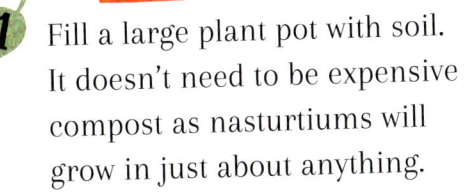

1. Fill a large plant pot with soil. It doesn't need to be expensive compost as nasturtiums will grow in just about anything.

2. Poke holes with your finger (about 2 cm deep and 10 cm apart).

3. Drop a seed into each hole, then cover it lightly with soil. Water in well.

4. After about 5–12 days, the seeds will germinate and leaves will appear soon afterwards.

5. They should flower after about a month.

6. Harvest the flowers, or dead-head them when they die, and you should get flowers all summer long.

SUNFLOWERS

Sunflowers are a brilliant plant to grow in your garden as they attract bees and insects and add spectacular bursts of colour. The seeds of the fully-grown sunflower also make excellent bird food. Sunflowers can be grown in pots in a sunny space and are best sown in April and May.

YOU WILL NEED:

- Small plant/yoghurt pots
- Compost
- Sunflower seeds
- Garden canes and string

SEASON Spring & summer

TIME 2-3 months

ENVIRONMENT Outdoors

HOW TO GROW:

1. Fill your pots with compost. Poke a small hole in the middle with your finger – it needs to be 1-2 cm deep.

2. Drop a seed in each hole, cover them with compost, then water well. Continue to water them when the compost feels dry.

3. After 1-2 weeks, you should begin to see shoots. When the plants grow too big for the pots, you can transplant them into larger pots or plant them out in a sunny garden spot.

4. As they grow, you will need to support them with garden canes. Tie the stalks loosely to the canes so that they don't get damaged.